Azad Ashim Sharma offers us something very unique in *Ergastulum*. The torrent of his disciplined yet melodic poetry does not only travel with forceful grace. Rather, his aesthetic precision and uncompromising craftsmanship cut through with elegantly disorienting eloquence: love, anger, sadness, substance abuse, race, labor, and revolt, only to unbind and bind them tightly in a politics of the poetic that weaves through London, Palestine, and Kashmir. Passionate, brilliant, lyrical, and affective, *Ergastulum* will be known for having established Azad as undoubtedly one of the most complex and talented poets of his generation.

— Stephen Sheehi, *Camera Palaestina: Photography and The Displaced Histories of Palestine*

Ergastulum may be named for a type of dungeon, but the bars of print on Azad Ashim Sharma's pages are placed to let in a lot of light. Held, but not contained, by the bonds of coronavirus sociality, Azad gives us a poetics of touch as luscious as an apricot, as frustrating as a trip to a closed zoo, as complex as quantum entanglement, and as vitally common as sweat. What names might this lit writing call to mind? Nuar Alsadir, Holly Pester, Christine Brooke-Rose, Jean-Luc Godard…philosophy, precarity, allusion and absurdity…yes, but also the release of dance and the struggle of revolution; Abt Vogler, Robert Browning's organist, improvising till he touches on the C major of this life. To assent to ascent, drag the scentless, traverse the senseless: Azad really does sing the body electric, decolonizing the refuge we find in the -ing, in the Verb.

— Vahni (Anthony Ezekiel) Capildeo, *Like a Tree Walking*

Breaking away from itself 'as soon as representation [is] afoot', *Ergastulum* is writing as afference, theory as incantation, lyric as charnel ground. These lines are virtuosic and macaronic, elaborating resistance within confinements of time that are conditionally funded or else endlessly applied for. Viscerally attuned to the touch of distance and the haptics of grammar, *Ergastulum* is a bibliomantic luminary – emptying itself out towards the hope of both 'another confidant' and the 'global public', which is to say, love.

— Daisy Lafarge, *Life Without Air*

Azad Ashim Sharma's *Ergastulum* is the anahaptic diagnosis of these pandemic times: screens hum, containers buzz, and the world's supplies chain the commons. Wrestling with the grammar of enemy territory and the constraints of the settler's diction, Azad sings the constant unmaking of our asocial cohesion. Against a world where phenomena bury the lyric body, these poems are armed with guerrilla ontologistics: picking up, moving forth, and grasping back out. In anticipation of the fight back, Azad's lines spit acts of recapture: weaving a poeisis from among the breaches of memory, holding down bays of relief for new modes of arrival, garnering strength to break back in and break shit back the fuck up. Lights out. It was in predictive predilection for the future acts of poetry that 'we razed the containment and embraced the coming horizon.' Finding each other in the dark, the colony is yet to crush this love.

— Ed Luker, *Other Life*

Lost time, no time, in search of lost time. Azad's *Ergastulum* packs a punch worthy of Marcel Proust. Only this time there's no time and the lack of meaning in the world is the result of living at work. Being thrown into a pit, like the slaves of old. The lack of contact. The sheer inhumanity of a world in which some humans can impose the destruction of life and world on time itself. 'We are out of touch with time itself', he tells us in the very first verses of this collection. But we also 'syncopate together', 'maroon in nanoseconds', and 'rave-rub against each other' until the spark is ignited. This is not just poetry, but lightning. And it is ready to set the world on fire. So that it can be reborn. Time, and time again. This is not just poetry, but lightning.

— Oscar Guardiola-Rivera, *Night of the World 1*

ERGASTULUM:

Vignettes of Lost Time

Azad Ashim Sharma

Also by Azad Ashim Sharma

POETRY:

Against the Frame, (Barque Press, 2017)

Today Young Veteran Walks with Bluebells on the Tricontinental Road,

(Earthbound Press, 2020)

ISBN: 978-1-915079-01-5

The author/s has asserted their right to be identified as the author of this Work in accordance with the Copyright, Designs and Patents Act 1988

Cover design by Aaron Kent

Edited & Typeset by Aaron Kent

Broken Sleep Books (2022)

Broken Sleep Books Ltd
Rhydwen,
Talgarreg,
SA44 4HB
Wales

Contents

Poetry is the opposite of algorithms.

– Luke Roberts

ERGASTULUM:
Vignettes of Lost Time

Azad Ashim Sharma

for callie gardner

NOTES OUT OF CONDEMNATION TO SENSE

"We've all heard endlessly about call and response, endless repetitions having to do with "community," "dialogue," so on and so forth. What I'd have us listen for and hopefully hear beneath the by now triteness of such observations, however, is a heretofore fallow reserve of poetic suggestion. It's not that we don't rightly hear call and response as both solicitation and bestowal of communal assent. Nor am I suggesting the chorus not to be a projection of sanction, a bodying forth of collective accord and/or insinuation. What I'm proposing is that we hear into what has up to now only been overheard (if I can put it that way), that we can awaken resources whereby, for example, *assent* can be heard to carry undertones or echoes of *ascent* (*accents* of ascent)."

– Nathaniel Mackey, *From A Broken Bottle, Traces of Perfume Still Emanate.*

The funding channels appear blocked and hopeless,
as hopeless as can be in this uncertain time of writing.

What is required is now some way to bullshit through the
application procedures, to search for financial goals.

In the hope of completion,
I have drafted some potential research questions:

What compels people to risk their lives collectively in the face of
injustice?

&: How does such feeling take hold?

They provoke me during the lockdowns and as witness to the false
starts of political insurgencies.

Another question forms:

Is there a pure collective feeling that passes through people who
are isolated from each other, socially distant, locked away by
necessity?

I'm spent now,
        longing for another confidant,
attempting to empty myself out
                        into a collective lyric we. I struggle.

In the UK, it is well reported

    that the lockdown has caused
        a spiralling decline
            in the population's mental health.[1]

One might be able to list causes:

isolation, alienation, lack of face-to-face communication,
limited mobility, increased screen time
        due to work moving 'online'

or the feeling that we are not working
from home but, rather, living at work, etc.

Such plethora of causes lead, ultimately, to a single experience:
                the lack of human contact.

We have fallen out of touch

with ourselves in the process of moving

our social lives online,   we have lost touch with

our loved ones, and,

with the foundation of reality itself,

    our sensorial faculty,   our means

by which we make the world around us accessible to perception.

We are out of touch with time itself, floating

    around like de-temporalised particles

from one point to another in a life

    quantified in the excess of its duration.

We don't have time to waste

    despite the earth telling us to slow down.

Lockdown –

we feel gripped by something other than ourselves

or the gaze or touch of someone we love;

    we are held by a virus, something we cannot see,
by emergency rules and laws. In this hold, we feel contained;

and, to be held and contained by something outside of ourselves
requires of us, in order to fully understand it, a certain capacity

for slowness, for dwelling,
in the midst of being held,
in the hold that contains.

        It is suffocating to lack a time,
a right time to feel oneself existing through,
                without the promise of completion.

Every day we shame each other with fitness videos from home.

    We are tired; we don't feel safe; we seclude.

If the lockdown gave us the private–self,
and the private–self's private–property,

    to cushion ourselves in containment,

that recourse to privacy is overthrown by haptic socialities:

insurgent collective feelings.

Kashif Sharma-Patel writes:

    We believed our self-hoods and then
        remembered it's a crock of capitalist
        shit.[2]

DEFERRED EMBRACE
(A journal entry from July 2020)

"Each of us is a descendent of those who not only stood upright and developed tools and language but also realised the importance of nonnarcissistic love. Narcissistic love seeks mirrors. Political love offers no such flattery, self-indulgence, and gratification. The future is never *ours*. It is a love always committed to the life and freedom of others."

– Lewis R. Gordon, *Freedom, Justice, Decolonisation.*

The sun blazes with acharnement; the air over the Imperial War Museum park sits too close for comfort; sweat clings to the skin, adsorptive, holding itself with a muggy stillness. Sweat emits, emanates, whispers of lovers, trickling into one another, a film of connection over tissue and sinew, bones that caress the tarmac with insistency and indeterminacy. It remembers friends who long for each other's embrace but cannot, because to socialise now is to be distant from one another, even if only by one-metre-plus.

Plants and trees sweat; a thin layer of translucence on leaves, the moisture of the bark, the slightly damp chitters of a squirrel with an acorn. The ascent to contact yearns with lost longing, directionless; a wave goes up and down, there is no movement forwards or backwards, no breeze to ventilate, no aeolian relief. The crowds are already a little dispersed, trudging against aestivation; exchanges of glances replacing the tact of palms or chests or elbows. They share hand sanitiser instead of letting their clammy cotton come into a mutual fold. Each spray a parody of the virus, its flocculent transfer.

Top lips sweat under masks, something no one can see, the expression of the mouth, no smiling or smirking, no frowning or pursing, just a mass of cloth emitting sonic vibrations that compete for space with perroquets and the echoes of traffic. In stillness too, there is a liquiform murmur; an excretion of temporality, the remainder, the reminder of what it was like before, what it would be like if things were not this way, distant yet overbearing like acedia, like hypaesthesia. What echoes is not the traffic of now but the traffic of then; it arches in consecution, back into the roar it once was, haunting space-time like the metatheses of hiccoughs or drunken laughter that lurk in the, now closed, Hercules pub by Lambeth North station.

Today, I am a lotus-eater; tomorrow, a gadabout, abscising my leftover creative enthusiasm to write. I linger between stops, silences, susurrations, hesitant like the bead of sweat rolling down my back as July welcomes me home, to the city I know from its edges, the indistinct line where the grass rests one-metre-plus from the concrete.

–

Kashif opens their front door and I yawp with the stupid comfort that they are still alive, that they aren't a statistic on the news. Anuka peers over Kash's shoulder, their shaved head bouncing into view like a tennis ball before a serve, but this one has specs and an assuring smile.

Like the air, we are suspended over time; in the space where contact should be, our eyes make the gesture, warming the distance between us; we are afferent together, at the points of a deconstructed triangle, lingering in the awkward hesitancy of the distance, against the patio, against the iron gate, under the scaffolding, we are there together, apart but connected by the air and its stifling stillness.

I tell Kashif and Anuka how I've missed them and ask about their health.

"Covid is a proper bastard," Kashif says.

"I've just been *so* tired all the time, and then occasionally I think I've got fever again…sorry, I'm still in my gown, I'm having one of those days; my depression has been hard to manage this week," Anuka says.

I light a cigarette, hand Kashif an envelope, tell Anu I'm sorry and ask them both if they'd like to walk.

"What's in this? Dhanveer's book? And yeah sure let me just put some shoes on I'll be down in a second. Can't be too long, Anu's mum is teaching me German, got a lesson in a coupl'hours and I ain't done my homework init." Kashif says.

I acknowledge the questions with affirmation from widened eyes and Anu says they'll join us later.

"Let me get my shoes" translates from Kashif to English as "let me totally change my outfit" and they come back down looking regal. With their grandmother's gold earrings dangling against their jet black mane and long beard, gold trainers to match, shorts and a white tank top, they move towards me like the future.

–

We make our way through the sweltering day, swanning through the backroads around Elephant and Castle, through red brick council estates, shooting the breeze about what books we've been reading, our recoveries, theirs from the virus, mine from addiction.

It is our first meeting since the lockdown began. We find a new freedom, a new comfort in being together, and the embrace of glances turns into the exchange of laughter; work comes up and Kashif informs me that they're feeling up to coming back. As we pass a hidden German bar on the approach to Vauxhall, I dictate a quick to-do list for them via voice-note to review later.

The sweat on my brow remains in an adsorptive state, stuck there, unable to move; the reminder of contact and the moist film across it, my own lake Manasarover on my forehead. There is no distinction at this point between individual droplets, each in touch through their distance, as one, as sweat and not as 'sweats' or 'drops of–'.

"You wanna check out the zoo?" Kashif asks.

"There's a fucking zoo?!"

"Yeah boss, just by Vauxhall park, it's jokes, bare llamas and goats."

As cobbled stones flatten into the arid park lawn, the llamas and goats come into view, their bleating pierces the stillness, moving the air in a cursive, the sun slightly out of view, the shade holds a dank oolong-like odour.

Kashif walks up to the Rasta outside the entrance, who explains that the zoo is closed today. This devastating news pushes us into the park and we walk past small gatherings, mainly couples enjoying the sun, people tanning, getting pissed, smoking weed.

We find a spot, near the sandy turf some fellas are using to play charades. An old white geezer in a straw fedora, wearing all white linen, is teaching a young black man – tracksuit bottoms, no top, a small side bag – how to play, emphasising the trick of throwing the ball with back spin. Their hands are loud with it; the game; the jouissance; the *gudunk* of the metal arrested by the grit.

"How the fuck are certain man out'ere tanning in their Y-fronts like they in Marbella?" I ask Kashif in a crude dialect of Hindi.

Kashif chuckles as I pass them a bottle of water from my rucksack. Behind the charades is a football-basketball hybrid court. A multipurpose steel cage. A group are inside, kicking ball, shooting hoops, blasting afro–beats, everyone in athleisure.

"It's good to see you though big man, was worried about your relapse and then obviously this coronavirus hungama has fucked up everything. How's your dissertation coming along?"

"It's not coming mate. I'm struggling with grasping (ha) Moten's concept of hapticality, struggling to write this creative-critical style. It's all a fuckery at the moment, to be honest. Bare stress."

"Oh is it? That's tough. Us poets tryna write prose. Or maybe that's why we write poetry, because we can't be fucked with prose."

"Aha! Yeah, probably; I just get frustrated, prose feels so policed, like show–don't–tell then tell–don't–show, then all this bullshit about fucking over–narrating. I swear you 'tell a story' and don't 'show a story' init; what the fuck is all this advice about. But yeah, it's pissing me off, frustrated; equally frustrated with not getting PhD funding. I feel like I don't want to even write the dissertation to spite the fuckers who didn't give me the money to study more."

"I'm sorry boss; that's proper shit. I know you worked so hard. I just wonder if it's because you ain't got the masters yet, init, things are so weird at the moment. Don't give up. Listen, I just remembered something about hapticality, init.

"Yeah, so, Moten came to Brighton, maybe a year or so ago, was jokes – obviously because Dhanveer knows him so we all got pissed with him after. But, yeah, he was talking about hapticality and it being like knowledge, hmm, maybe not production but let's say that, so knowledge production, but like, in the undercommons init, so not in this formal assessment bullshit. Literally like, how the fuck we live with thought and people and affect. And then Moten basically went on to talk about why football (obviously my–man said Soccer, init) is better than basketball. And like, basically the gist of it is, he loves Messi; says Messi is a poet of hapticality."

"The ball is always in motion, part of the body, always at risk of taking the wrong turn because the ground's surface is unpredictable. In basketball, you hold the ball, so you remove the variables. The variables are what makes hapticality, hapticality. And basically because it's the neologism yeah, of haptic and sociality, he then starts going on about the Messi-ness of sociality. It was jokes."

"Is there a recording?" Kashif informs me that these things ain't ever recorded and that you just gotta be there.

I light another cigarette. Someone in the court is practising free-kicks; he shoots, and the back of the cage rattles. The others start singing *"Top baller, top baller, put it in the top corner"*. [3]

"That's the point init, hapticality." Kashif says, turning to me, their eyes smiling.

–

AFTER TOUCH

"How to touch upon the untouchable?" Jacques Derrida asks.[4]

Sometimes you receive a call and you have to reply.

I could answer Derrida,
    & talk about the socially distant crowd;

it is the representation of contact amidst the failure of connection.

People move in proximity, at the limit of new coronaviral sociality, and the "[l]imit is not to be touched," it "steals away at a touch, which either never attains it or trespasses on it forever."[5]

My answer is sweat; the slickness which keeps askance two surfaces trying to connect; the spray of hand sanitiser or the greeting of eyes (above masks) instead of the embrace, the handshake, the kiss.

Social distancing is uncomfortable not solely because of the pandemic, but because it is the biopolitical manifestation of "the haunting of touch."[6]

Derrida would ask some further questions and they could be simplified as follows:

What is going on in touch? If touch moves and affects what it effects, what happens in the quantum dimension, what happens at the level of the untouchable?

–

I reach out to the keyboard,
my fingers and the keys
mutually repel each other,
forcing the keys in, inscribing   the page,
and in that inscription another
line of force all the way from   the tips
of my fingers through my arms
into my spinal column,   to my brain.

I sense myself at the desk, typing with affirmation.

I want my body to be a phenomenon;
I want it to be able to grasp and hold the world;

I want to acquire a name in history;

I want to come into view for myself
but a mirror's image is just that – a mirrored image.

Myself flipped and distorted,
elusive to my own view
from my window (my eyes)   out of reach, intangible.

—

I pause and my hands leave the keys, holding each other, hands in hands. How close are they? As close as myself?

> Perhaps closer. And if the two hands belong to one person, might this not enliven an uncanny sense of the otherness of the self, a literal holding oneself at a distance in the sensation of contact, the greeting of the stranger within?[7]

Barad's research in quantum field theory, physics, and touch, is other-worldly. Barad takes us beyond the classical physics of Democritus, beyond the mere assertion of electromagnetic rejection, into the void of (my) self (the stranger within) and into the distance that both holds and collapses in this sensation of contact.

The electrons in my fingers are immoral, perverse, they do not function according to easily calculable laws and measurements. They are erratic, indeterminate, infinities that multiply. What happens when two electrons are brought together is "an infinite number of possibilities," "an infinite sum over all possible histories."[8] They interact in the space around them with "virtual particles," the "ghostly non/existences that teeter on the edge of the infinitely fine blade between being and nonbeing."[9] If this is hard to grasp, it is because grasping the quantum field is by nature of its matter and material, ungraspable, unthinkable, but thinking and grasping are still contained there.

Touch is troublesome because at the quantum level we are no longer talking about surfaces coming into contact but rather "*touch touching itself.*"[10] At this quantum level, every instance of touch "is itself touched by all possible others" all times, dimensions, matters.[11] To be touched is to be touched by touch itself and to touch is to touch touch itself. What was once tautology represent indeterminate ontologies, pluralised and multiplied flows of matter, of material, through the body, that the body is made of and that lives and breathes and thinks with and as the body.

[Derrida's...]

Thinking is a material matter:

> Thought experiments are material matters. Thinking has never been a disembodied or uniquely human activity.[12]

Touch affirms that I do not know what my body is made of, what matters; at this level, I touch myself as a stranger. What we experience in thinking about touch as a spectral absence of touch is the indeterminacy of virtual particles, electrons, photons, small pieces of matter that contain in them, infinities:

> Even the smallest bits of matter are an unfathomable multitude.[13]

This theory of 'touch as touch touching itself' enters, embraces, approaches the matter-real level of ontological indeterminacy, radical openness, an infinity of possibilities. Part of that is not the affirmation of the self through a body schema but a perspective of the alterity within the self as part of, made of, and in a dynamic play with matter itself. Repulsion at the heart of attraction; rejection at the heart of contact; infinities at the quantum limits of the electromagnetic sensation we know as touch, the alterity within as we attempt comprehension of the self without.

—

Open both hands at the same time. Say a prayer. Rub your palms over your face.

STEP*PING*
TO THE LEFT
OF ONTOLOGY

Harness the power of quiet.

– Jazmine Linklater, *Future Notes Towards an Alternative: a manifesto.*

Irreverent diagrammatic anaximander

a note

stowed away I was —

had had a feeling

Time ends and began in the innards –

peristaltic progress negating

auto-affective   peregrinations

Trapezoid buoyed

to rest in fallacy –

active forgetfulness it would be

fun if not for the proviso —

We were signs taken by wonderment

We were starts hastened to fall down —

Should be astral travelling

with moons around —

our elbows   famed attraction

A mess   missives   midrift

of planks

over the wall

we are whimpering foxes in the quarry ——

The yogi asks me to get back to my breathing

it is illegal
to not obey metaphysics
    our search for de-ontologised   </futures>

against our knowledge
    that we've been locked
in the death of time
    its scentless performances

of accelerated information
& whizz-banged task management
we sought out the minor
doors towards the horizon
where we could become changelings.

Reduction to loam
                                    we could be [
   proto-grammatologues I see you

deferring and differing the shake of the task
of the task in the trace of misery beams

Suddenly to be cockneyed / a chicken-by-bow type
of situation eggs the question on basic demands

four bare necessities: live, laugh, love, let-go.]

we all tried humour
doing the Einaudi
on a make shift ice shelf —

    Existenz is paused

to be free in the ruin or to hold the popul vuh
following the guidance to re-allegorise the allegory –

Held close in the water
saying flowed between repulsions of skin

which we were feeling as a quantum moment
of contact just to be unthinkable and thinking

——   we address the constraints

trying to reckon with the rekhet in rechtsphilosophie
the waves of acid in an ocean of mitochondria

——   or druids from our inner polis

We were trying to hold each other outside of time.

Far off shall we go
            to decolonise normative living
    with anti freeze
                    on my armpit hair
and an oven glove
    on my left hand when it speaks in ink

</RX>

    it is never done but stays in the saying

To write poetry is to move into the air
</   resist nihilism's endgame of deracination
    & to address you in poetry
    with and as endless spelling errors
                                    />

    abreactive code for dissent
    melismatic ostinato of mantric wove

we syncopate together in what subtends
as a quotidian readerly poetics
    we take notes when words make worlds for us
and we moved in concrescence / –

    somewhere over the hill it was so easy

then the red tape was placed over our thumbs. />

We acknowledged a mutual respect for books
the pages of which we were rendered unable to turn

our mouths taped over with read as we tried to utter
the unutterable protest against the anti-protest receipts. />

Of tongues   macaronic (
          before we sought flexion in

such ebullient fractal
                    interiors   weren't-ever-fully-ness
to remain curious is to be provoked in the best way

through all this maelstrom or death
of thought   is another -ology
                                        </sAA>

The state of apology – and we were chained
          in and by it
~~ergastulum~~
to speak of and at the threshold of the haptic

Asiatic negritude to unmake thingifications
wilt to knowledge
          deserts in the sky
                              [Braithwaite's breath waits]

yes the impulse to meander
          or circumvent gangrenous landlords

demiurgic non-compliance —
pessimism as epistemic decay

Houseplants wiggle in the draft
offering critiques in face of dust
/ supervenes the regulatory board
defined as juridical flowers
      resting on the succulent globe

détourne />

      the object from prefatory withdrawal
a teleological suspension of the poetic
to get back at the sutured essence
      take the leap into the grey
growth felt as an implosion
      it was not meant to be like this
we were made to be held together —

Democratic abscissions of the spectacle
      to be human is to be untimely
to be post human is to recover semblance
      it may not always be the best thing going
but sometimes it is necessity that prompts us in movement

To be on the laterality/
shifting the geography and its psyche of ~~Dasein~~
      •   it means to break through the sign continuum
go! to the future where exchange is oxygen–

To've been in spirit like barbiturated sharks
in the bi-odyssey of race liberalism
put out of play
                    (tideialectics)
    we were marooned in or by sub-
marination   compressed into nanoseconds
                we risked life's in-plosive of the *is*
                        closing presence in the pensive

failure in the moment of articulation
        lock arff'd in meta critique
burdened or limited by manhood as irreplaceable

Or in the mansion of absence
golden guild of legalised pocket collars
whence mystic writing pads a-shore.

Careless egological sense faculties
 giving little-*a* an economy or a chemistry

thorough or rough we went there
though we thought in the going of it
life was in and of a slant
 a gap   an interstice
at an impasse
 quoting each other by chance
scilicet orthogonal
 rust in urbane plisséd mauve skein

& you and I everyday
   virology visits periastron of diphthongs

                                                      —

   the self in the care praxes collections
Having been or will become the had of

≠

   anonymous textuality predicates endeavours
devours or descends into the scene of

                                                      —

   variations of silent monologues
alien material that doing the explanation with

[
   some scene of the de-construct
left in the waning b-line there was

   a problem that could be conditional
urine alchemical proffering to latitude

                                                      ]

   wherein forged was the rhapsodic
decreation in the pharmakon

+

   Śūnyatā moves in promethean prolegomena
in the struggle of continuation

                                                      </

   where we took it all too seriously in the grip
to move passed cherry-picking which samples we're in.

In the meniscus </of your knees
               closure became indefensible [

—

    swines without spines
                           bam!
                           bam!
;   goes the annoying fly
                    towards
</
       />

    the undead sociality,

we should talk about it

    that we know what we are in
    in our attempts at undoing it

troubadoric modal complaint

    that we were undone by it
    as soon as we felt it's space

(having been about to fall in the opening of your eyes
    [indefatigable and indecent homines sacri

Wondered wherein
we were of   Southern Kemet
in search of the opening of
                              </ka

          at the moment where beyond justice
seemed fated
          occurrent of worldliness and of world loving
we the people wondered
          into and of the same
whereof   [
          the burlesque style

     ]
                    Love is the form of the global public
reclamations exist
          in queerness   where we were all in a traced origin
chasing to stand apart or there apart from
          to breathe
          is not to work
refuge in the -ing
                              hubbub in the roads
a repartee as the decks turn over portable as sound
esurient for a nutritional stupefacient i.e. the dance

                    </no sa7/>

we broke away as soon as representation was afoot
Fuckery at hand cause duppy know who to frighten—

Played truant   w./ austere pre

    positions-

spurious and

    ■ under-valent w.o./ disclosed unity

as lacking sovereign or soft thinking
wherever we are or will come to on arrival

schema of indecision
    I was saying I love you / said you felt it too
I wonder when we will meet again ~~[saying]~~
    but for now to have digitality between us
plugs the others into each contact / con tact

    ■ dismantling the reconstitution of identity

wrong overturn in the beyond right principality of
    something known as a wipe off boot
mud over the flecks of shadowed embrace

Is played truth and sea
in the abyss of prudence
    not to be contrary
stitched crossed hairs out of navel graspin'–

Bumblin   were we in the ono-matter
like bees in the middle of rosemary flowers
absorbing vial-lilac incepting with or as off-beat

having melted the trees we were not
in a position to retrain that thought

- wound up in the colon as globules of liver spots

To have bumbled in trudging through an arch-way –

Under-ray of the apricot sun's aura-glow
an oracular function on low theories
entangled roots post decay off–on the in-step'd sentience

fleshy with it like rhubarb we could smell
fingers jostling for the rub and feel of it

- was something having been not possible
to be synthesised a-priori but remain in occultation

- Stood over each working through each other

non-phonically by an alleyway to the cobbled street
- in a narrow dé-onto- without theodicy

In recognition came smatterings of ethernet potential
given over to hyletic as opposed to the transcendental.

To say we are before matter

a   divulgence of thought
non-separable from the inhale
whence exhalation yielded a reference

Held in the experiment
          it would've been called
declivity or in the interoceptive focus
          electrolytic earth
damned to be in the wretch of it

retro-kinetic in harmolodic stutters
that was where it came unto be seen and conquered

]
          magnetic strata of the out-flow
]

          called you and you'd been all expecting me

]
          bibliomancers with intentions hark to not-yet
sub-epidermal reals as morphs of conjunction

                              </conjecture>

In the rue we row in parallel
it was the end of eschatology

[anonymity]

   —

    In-roads made of fallen statuettes
    maybe it happened to enter newness

      (saying is the trace of said)

   —

Sufism of straddled threads and resisted in-shackling

</sa7>

   felt the Simurgh on our patch
   work denim and therein slept

  Home was never outside the minds
  or found stilled in our hopeless flesh:

Puissant police handled   / masked on-lookers–

Vertigo   felt like a hike

                                    towards

on-going-ness   </.>   numbingly
~~silent~~

        a ripple effect
        rippling affect

        shuttling off the dream-works

</?>   Projects coming in line with the gas pipe
        shouting at a telegraph pole building site

                    </!>... a fucking mess

Hypertext oriented

                    in the league of genteel fascism

Stop   /   ping!

end   to reconsider

                balance   tilt to the right

appease the pitchforked pride

                    wasting away in fever.

Aubade
for the perform-attic assembly not thrown
         into the road   or it was to be
caught extended   and wrapped in bills
                                 [

a classic wash in canned food for worms
                                 [

in normal circumstances we cannot be
hand in hand raising voice
                        to hold to account
now we feel the compression   [
—   [
condensations on bulletproof glass we were
trying to get to the other side of the bridge
with our friends but it felt like discrimination

</to be successful

Weathered we were whittled

                       down by truncheons
in the constitutive exclusion

        of our notation towards
further elaboration />

                       without –

In excess of said
　　　　pre-discursive it was felt

plural forms or styles
　　　　we disobeyed received iconography

what amounts of death we wouldn't live with.

</sa7> —

Exit strategy meetings
　　　　minutes of small scales

records on shuffle blithering
　　　　paperless bricolage(s) palpable yet new clear

rarities – it was the wage as form we were up against.

　　　　　　　　　　　—

Singularities of percentile incense
　　　　did not have to forego

these opportunities
　　　　perhaps we underestimated

a majority share in the nomenclature / gnome culture.

In their brackets
                    we were plied
or splayed
                            to be reverent
to the display
        or highly defined

        Could not have
        foreseen or foretold
                /
        it breaks back
        along the current

disassociation /   Heartlessness

to say what has been said
                all of its vanity

        expunged in total denial
[A-Chiasmic to not signify the para-de-onto-theological]
~~]lacigoloeht-otno-ed-arap eht yfingis ton ot cimsaihC-A[~~

Undefined as people
                we entered the less as stately

        Over determined as things
                        we left our rights with them

Come to over stand that fear of and fear for are not equal

Our attempts at embodiment   \</of deixis>

fell into the abyssal bind   regaled double

~~consciousness~~   floating precarity hurt
ling a nuisance in the acting of it
                         we came understood as–

We turned our poems over the xerograph
                                   \</this>

was how we caused annoyance or serious harms

and the region should suffer us as we suffer its sentence

\</that>
                    we acted on and off inchoate coexistent

[out of deictic]

to escape   secutarian attrite macabre rhyme-them

acceleration would be death but to think slowly

\</of this/that>   makes of a person a ~~people~~.

FOR
GIVING
(ELSA'S SPIRIT)

"Diasporic consciousness develops an ethic of generosity."

– Nathalie Etoke, *Melancholia Africana.*

; What we needed was not the same as wanting
but it made for better refusal of unpayable debt

[

; to be forgiven or having received for-giving-ness
much ado in the late spring to mislay a claiming

]

; not to be emptied or excavated by remonstration
had forced a defence of poetry out of the songs

[

; popular calls tort restitution flabbergasted aroma
or it was an arrhythmia apposite to the disclaimer

]

; broader feeling over the sink of realism rose up
alabaster overtures in euromodern surplus good

[

; disgust abound won't surfeit for purpose things
we felt the urge to put our heads through the walls

]

; may've awoken to claret blue dusk in the suburbs
sat on the edge we realised it was not so optimistic

[

; to live in paper and its texture in flight from logic
we became universal individuals by not partaking

]

; in the measure we weren't commiserated or razed
& — we heard each other kicking through the earth

–

Might be
        popping out
            of a break
don't sort it all out   so quick
chained by the hip
        pissed on   ripped steel

through the air like a hiss /
        through the air with a kiss
we broke the door off the hinge
                & havin' been more
than honest a beer and a spliff
in crystal palace working through
        it subsists on degenerating
                    our flesh into objectives

                        *

I never learnt because my skin was burnt
        from a rhythm that was in my solar plexus
            like nerve endings in sinew
to be broken and rebuilt by and with you
I felt reformed or re-issued /now our spines are upright
all the conservatives are uptight
with lips looking like steel girders covered in fireflies
We broke free together ; we were up for the fight
We pissed on the Inglish field;   "it's over like 1979."

</Fuck the analysts> post-lad poly-culture
ready to do sub-fraud origametre
of poems swang like a blade in the z-fold
wrote a big lyric-We:—
told them sad boomers to freshen up freshen up
policemen looking anxious all tense up tense up
spud to the real ones it was all bless up bless up
why you so threatened by us when we á rise up

<end the analysing/> ~~ring the alarm~~

convinced you an index 'n' middle digit was a hand gun
why you so threatened by us when we just ah hold hands?

[road poetics] not dealt in memoir about brown bugaboos

We won't sell out ~~family~~ for pay we won't work against ~~family~~
again ~~family~~ is extension of affect in the dungeon don't write
about ~~family~~ to assimilate. [Revitalisation, yeah] It was summer
when we'd fully inhaled. We wrote poems to spread hydration
and by the poems of others we were hydrated.

Every exhale we pushed were takhalluses

+

we reached the point of recognition, it was late.

:

Lazy modernists we turned into by the backroad quays.

</

On the page we made good first hand impressions.

/>

We bobb'd our heads like serpents out a wicker chamber.

=

Tennis'd our elbows under the blaring square waves.

—

Voices gruff from wheeling up the interior modulation.

[

Did close reading in the pause before we fell into it.

]

We woke up to the vibes and let them work through us.

+

Our teeth were licked by the acid-talk of what we spat.

=

In the open air we broke the tick of the second hand.

(

Pheromones circulated in sonoluminescencing dum-da

—

Ferral moans un-reticulated in the phonotactic tirikitté-ta

;

& beats indexed by our flesh silvered in sun conscience–

[We don't ever want to come around]
    but to remain in the over-flight
        away from mobility exercises–

It was attempted to turn our curiosity
    into a state of incarceration
        to steal from our health-spans

There was a drought of aesthetics
    every other one of us was recourse
        and identity became de-punked

[We decided we didn't like this anymore]
    Having felt a neck crack we wrote
        to each other in the subconscious

Preferring balance to symmetry we were opposed
    or placed in that o-o-o-position
        but we met these failures with refusal–

[Likened to a transportation beyond the pulse]
    like cans we sprayed the walls with design
        pumping up the valium we grafted–

Back in the deep we met the paranoia otherwise
    we could touch our feet again
        rolled over the loss of care [so it seemed]

In a tower-block semi
-detached from rurality
We met each other   / sang together

Our eyes wearied
writing into the screen
          thirsty for poems

                              / Some combination

of liquidity as sound-systemic
          we made sunset musicals
a combination of mad-sad proto-org*a*sms
turned freytag pages with heron-like raspiness

</original piracy /
          lovembracèd material jouissance/>

and whence guided by Guido Qawwalcanti
we desired each other / were desired by each other.

From a vantage where
                              the city looks
          small   and spikey
                       we were
                       our love children
                                        never returning / to the same.
—— How we did physiologically
              did not depend upon anteriority
or vita-mineral formations in the cups
                              from which we drank.
In a silent mood
we quickened over the slack /

                          and having regained or refuelled
in covert gyration to overstep
the remark to have had
blessing approach us in the breeze
over the balcony on the roof
the horizon lit up with the pink orb.

...dusty corduroy
              perched ever so
              slightly over
                       canvas hi-tops
The bass levelled us it was like a movie
or a journey or somewhere in between–
What we moved
              as in the dance
was swooned interpretation

reading aloud in each other's ears
in the ensuing set of shade
                                   / it was so lit.

Erring on the side of upcoming brilliance to only
have been consumed by </panic.> it was a trance-
like state of </overcoming/> what went into us

to write is to exitenz as [of] and [in] at the otherwise
quantum-similitude of long axes </to say is to subsist>
being part of our anguished ink-wishes as it was always.

Bear with me Lucretius we come [in] at the afterwards
singing our ghazals in cantos of guided vantage points
at the demi-verge of requisite remonstrata [we] desired

[out-of] remained in the foregoing of a ~~conclusion~~ for
faculties of deep dirt to find odd futures with fishy tones
how ~~grey~~ could the sky actually get <?> maybe more so

From down [;] we made it <./through> a break w./ love
where care becomes enmeshed with the politic of it all
not to be able to integrate the notations with the ~~draft~~

There w/ each other it came to be that the chainz didn't
hold much but a space we could exit into or from <!>
for they aren't always already the same in the first place

No python will build a ~~parthenon~~/ no country for tuna
Found ourselves toiled by the land we longed for oceans
we're made of astrologers who lived [airless] on comets.

Re-/processual über-thought

a touch of bad circulation {blue fingers}

some parabiology of kinship that awoke in and around us

[choice exits where fate enters]

</ & history forgets what it needs to re-member>

deep faked rhododendron

came through all mean and slimy

the big questions like ~~how~~ to live or ~~what~~ to stand by
seemed off when asked in conjunction t' / how are you?

We stayed put / lingering–

In the compressed uniformity
        deluged information
                rocked by the usurper / tricked by usage
Working is just a replacement
                        for signification
        I'm not so sure it's all going to be
okay, and is okay
                                enough?

In cartooned décolletage   [
   escapist phantasy
      oh you gripped me
         by that funny bone   ]

         walk with me a little while   —
         + where we forked by a lake
         tell me it will be okay
         because it's not meant to be this way.

I know that was what we spoke about but
   we've both got nerves
      </like arpeggios of semiosmosis>
         do me a favour and find the key.

         now bleeding on the water front
         then pounding on the door like
         this wasn't just a dressed rehearsal
         all we wanted was freedom – [

Softly into my ear you told me to pull up the blind
   and look onto the horizon
      make the world possible again]
         full of hope and levity
  but this mutual bondage of islanders
  as a water sign on a land with water people
  it ain't enough to try luck without prior planning–
We look at or to each other
     with wonder but it wasn't
in the same measure
     as the way we broke our chains   </>
all the salmon have chlamydia in Scotland
& we were disillusioned by the packaging

         –

Corrupted
      we evolved into having been fitted
                              for purpose
consent flew out
        the window when it came
                            to our assent
a grand narrative
          ace in the toad in the hold
                    lachrymal spawn
                        a magus of steadfast patience

[   ]

      we could not be a hundred percent
      sure of what we were in need of desiring
      it didn't feel right to want or need
      to have life dictated from the exterior
      the ungiven totality of abjection or endings.

In the pause of the break or the broken pause

[   ]   we suffered with each other

mentally unhealthy with the dolphins in Taiji

in competition with net rhizomes   [   ]

old conceptualisations of our topological urgencies

[   ]   proliferated in the time-reels

outside a not-yet hopescape of rigorous formations

learning to recognise blackface in reports [   ]

race became an old stale signifier and death was just

[   ]   the vainglory of the statisticians

like why do we need to accept this amount of destruction?

life put on some fucking stupid design   [   ]

catch one for the show and kill a hundred more

[   ]   we've become vehicles of greed –

A lyric eye is not as strong as its we-counter-whole. /
readied to be in community with people is not failure /
if it means less bread on the table in the short term /
the proposition is that we work towards a zone /
where these kind of concerns for basic amenities are /
superfluous and do not correspond with any debates /
the valorisations of our rights to exist and subsist /
within that are incontrovertible or indistinguishable /
from our base line affirmations of what the justice /
of tomorrow will look like in that we won't be held apart.

/ Appurtenance it's not really what we after anyways
/ back logs of streamlined sets of qualitative digressions
/ serving only to place in service of some stately vocation
/ we need more than what is on offer and want more
/ than is visible on the table you really can't give us morsels
/ having taken existenzial out of the zone of non-being
/ it was apparent that we should ride or die for its success
/ piety left us with holes in our jumpers and ripped jeans
/ a sequencer of the sort you witness in the gammon-être
to move relation out of discourse and into practice #scenes.

We were in the habit of   <./ having been
continued or lost in the habit   ./>

of having to wait for continuation
some kind of paradox where   ; we met [

past and future selves / halved ideas
of the self like offal thrown into the waste

;] we were tricyclic and afferent together
backed into the corner refusing to work again

Told you thrice not to fucking piss us off
not to fuck around by promising undelivered reals

but now we are left with a police boot on our turf
and the explosion may be coming </

if it is too hot in ergastulum, turn the fanon />

Odylic hypostatisation
        Lo t'was Humayun's tomb
with a chardi kala bad boy dub plate
        let it sing across this unregenerate archipelago
of unscented threshold feelings.

Ah yes the visitation of the pilgrims of duration
made our will to freedom a Right or even just Idea
&   we will endure in this life and the next.

Tomorrow will never come
at least not as expected
        but, we could become it
poēsis as the plain upon which we overcome pleurisy–

PANTECHNICON OF DYSCHRON CITY

1. Post-Internet Voyage

The Sein is static, we have said and continued in saying; this was also potentially a mistranslation from the Germanic script/ existence can and may've already been unintentional, something that / which we moved into. Para-signs are equally unintentional, flabbergastingly so, perhaps because they are just more illusion cast over our eyes or received as a radical image of alterity which will change us all. We began to lose the little patience we'd been holding dear all along. What this is all a part of is a machinic view of vanguardism which cannot be stowed away in monocultural aero-towers by the seaside. We have a movement ebbing between our soles and the ground.

Having had a feeling that the reason we'd come to understand those who are or were or will come to be in transition and/or the dysphoric amongst us whose comradeship meant a new world was possible where life was no longer a quantified peregrination but something opposed to the stasis of Hobbes' leviathan. Thus having been in cognisance of this comprehension, grasping, or even the rogue hand which knows how and when to hold onto affected matter; we have come here having had a feeling of being held by Idea and this was the inherent queerness of the Body.

From that we knew or were informed by the knowledge of exercise composing a mere fifteen percent of movement and that this was how the state's normalising algorithm wanted us to be and to make us believe that this lack of movement was the norm and everything else, our jerkiness and jitter-buggery would become shameful. Static was the air in Dyschron City which policed our mobilisations with a huge influx of soviet nootropics. We refused to ingest, inhale, initiate. This was received by the administrative members of society, doo-good-ing pen pushers of anonymous letters that moved through web 2.0 without any space-time affiliation, as a veering of our capacity to raise our toes in the splayed anthems of Not-Yet.

Sweet-Sweet-Poetry, the opposite to the statisticians' local anaesthetic tone, rested with us in the lingering space between our toes, where webbing once was, and it reminds us of an ocean. Transition: we're all in it / the rest of us who try to work with a body for a There / which is a willingness of Will / the future as Already-Been. We spoke to therapists and grandaunts of the 90s rave scene who had many scars to show for their achievements, all of whom were regaining the loss of time, or were in some sense of the word, guilty with separation anxiety, a manifesting of an out-of-sequence creature which found us after the end to be continued.

Hovering over was the engineering of ascent as dissent, across a bridge over a stream of possibilities. The event was not really an event in this zone of the eleventh cycle of Venus's rose, but a perennial without rest water feature in the southern aurora. Succession quickens against the reach. Temporality has consumed identity and the crises of both reduced to Only Now. Instructions to be present, to present our projects, to project our self-presentations, all linearity (read: nuance) was disallowed. And so we emerged in the vortex and the vortex was given its gravitation by our bodies.

Over the hurtling and under the hurting of post-Newtonian flight, we concurred to harness the centrifuge and its petrichor to move beyond the currents of (k)/now-ing and join together in little fingered chains of discontent. At the left of ontology we found orbis tertius, a ship sailing towards the Tlön, full of Uqbaric scrolls of unleavened bread made from grains upon which ink sat up-right. Fan out your nostrils, says the wind in the sail, shouts the parrot on the look-out ledge, and a clanging of drum taps from the *DAMPFTRIUMPHWAGEN* and then the motion and its re-scenting of the chronic worked through us, harmony from the irregular structures of our ligaments in this unformed shapeliness. The wagon took us away from the point, made the line a dot and the dot fade away into a horizon. Our eyes were refreshed by the hazy afterglow of effort, of strain, of experience. We'd finally come to a place of stillness which vibrated with history. We had reached the end to be continued.

2. Hsiang Yin and Thereafter.

It was There on the wave we saw it, a beautifully dense approaching of mist. We entered it and immediately felt dew wash our faces. Our new shipmates danced in the moist air, slowly, with grace, worldliness about their spirits, sealed in by the fragrance. Ash, Pine, Cedar, Moss, these were all mixed into the air's water, breath of the earth, life unbound and un-re-constructed. Our shoulders loosened, we were relieved by the gyrations, clicked our trunks, stretched upwards, outwards, to reach past the top of ourselves.

Our feet scrunched up in the inopportune memory of a poetics of grounding; all the while we drifted into a fluid time, casing out touch inwards. Held to the breeze whiling with smoked sea-spray like butterflies on water lilies; we had come to the collective grip; we redefined mysticism in the sealed humidity. Thin as rain; a cloud shower; an up-welling in the spring salination that lay over our salamander tongues; and we scurried across the deck looking There.

Misfits, outcasts, renegades; we'd been accused of not slowing down which we interpreted as envy of our need for thought to have continuity and a record of it in motion; so we progressed and opened ourselves to the droplets of reflections in a commitment to resting matutinal contemplation. No more fear of the wake and its obsession with re-presence. We pursued and were pursued by our traced pursuits; we razed the containment and embraced the coming horizon.

We experienced and were taken in by a phenomenal relief, a sense of latent love that seeped outwards from our teeth; no longer were we on exiled land where broadsheet publications announced the arrival of novels hailed as the love-children of Virginia Woolf and Frantz Fanon but which fell flat as bourgeois melodramas in a fancy suit, such bromide absurdisms were not present amongst the crew. Instead we heard the music of the torqued canvas sail, the ripple of water by the rudder, the creak of the wheel, the trudging towards unknown and unimagined peace. That was all we were after.

Made a beginning from an end, it was serene in the unfurling brume. There was no going back to ancillary ways, no regurgitation of nostalgic images of triumphant nationalism, and over us at the final moment of stillness before the Hsiang Yin dissipated was a yellow moon, a ring-less Saturn, the afterglow of solar wind. We stood together, looking up in acceptance. The seal of fragrance lifted and we saw our destination: Filastin.

3. The Dreams We Didn't Share

In the transdermal nicotine patch; my subconscious bazaar.

Belfast in the Summer by Gilmore is playing. I stand on the ground and my listless wavering perspective on the trades-people shouting is nauseating. I gag, in my sleep (?), deepening reflexes to disorientation. The crescendo; amen-break over the sunset, canvas flapping in the gentle breeze, touching me, curling

my chest hair / turns towards it, touches it, the breeze, breaking over the canvas sunset, the denouement.

A cry breaks out. I follow the commotion.

The world of the bazaar opens onto a stage. Play within a play, in a tent, in a bazaar. Cushion cover over a person's crown, jeggings, striped t-shirt. Another, 5 panel hat and large beard, shorter, stockier than the first, dressed in a red jumpsuit.

D Double E is dj-ing behind the stage, wearing a black t-shirt with white writing over his chest. It reads: haptic. He flicks up the fader and the amen-breaks resume with continuity. Two microphones descend from the ceiling like jellyfish. Someone in the crowd motions like a wheel in reverse. To reload; to rewind.

I blink and am back at the beginning, following the cry that broke out, walking (back) into the tent.

Roll the Dice by Shy FX now rumbles on, the gritty bassline, Lily Allen's smooth vocals, live inna the flesh.

Rude boy you seem like a smoker. Come we go chat shit on the sofa.[14]

She is singing to me. I close my eyes wishing I had dropped MDMA.

I open them to recognise the two on stage.

There's a whole world I wanna show you.[15]

The instrumental plays; they prick my ears.

Pablo Maurette:	The notion of the haptic includes touch understood in its literal and metaphorical sense and cannot be but thought alongside the tactile...[16]

Karl Marx: Therefore *all* the physical and intellectual senses have been replaced by the simple estrangement of *all* these senses – the sense of *having*.[17]

Pablo Maurette: ...but its artificiality, its impermeability, and its elasticity make of it an invaluable navigational instrument for whomever sets out to explore the ocean of tactility, of which skin is only the surface.[18]

Karl Marx: The supersession of private property is therefore the complete *emancipation* of all human senses and attributes; but it is this emancipation precisely because these senses and attributes have become *human*, subjectively as well as objectively...[19]

Pablo Maurette: (pardon my French) *la texture du texte*[20]

Karl Marx: The *senses* have therefore become *theoreticians* in their immediate praxis.[21]

The Crowd: Communism is the *positive* supersession of private property.[22]

In the rave we rub against each other and in the crowd we find commons in the session. I am blind skin; I am texture and surface.

I turn around to leave the tent worried my nicorette patch is coming off due to the positive accumulation of sweat in the crowd.

By the exit stands George Orwell, with his red notebook, scribbling down the prices of the commodities on sale, CDs, Vinyl, T Shirts, Beer. He is weighing them up against tobacco. He offers me a cigarette.

I show him the patch.

He stubs his cigarette out on it.

"Rude boy," he says, "you looked like a smoker."

[END]

Acknowledgements

The author would like to thank the editors of SPAMzine, Senna Hoy, and the Social and Health Sciences 2021 special issue "Necrocapitalism and Psychic Violence" for their publications and translations of short extracts from this work.

Endnotes

1. Schraer, Rachel, "Coronavirus: Severe mental health problems rise amid pandemic," *BBC* (12 August 2020) <https://www.bbc.co.uk/news/health-53742121> [accessed 12th September 2020].

2. Sharma-Patel, *Fragments on Mutability*, p. 4.

3. Wiley, "Top Baller," in *Boasty Gang – The Album* (London: Wiley Presents, 2020).

4. Derrida, Jacques, *On Touching – Jean-Luc Nancy*, trans. Christine Irizarry (Stanford: Stanford University Press, 2005), p. 6.

5. Ibid.

6. Ibid.

7. Ibid., p. 206

8. Ibid., p. 212

9. Ibid., p. 210

10. Ibid., p.212

11. Ibid.

12. Ibid., p.208

13. Barad, "On Touching–The Inhuman Therefore I Am," p. 214.

14. Shy FX, and The Sauce "Roll The Dice ft. Stamina MC & Lily Allen," in *Raggamuffin Reloaded* (London: Cult.ure, 2020).

15. Ibid.

16. Maurette, Pablo, *The Forgotten Sense* (London: The University of Chicago

17. Marx, Karl, "Economic and Philosophical Manuscripts (1844)," in *Early Writings*, trans. Rodney Livingstone and Gregor Benton (London: Penguin, 1992),

18. Maurette, *The Forgotten Sense*, p. 5.

19. Marx, "Economic and Philosophical Manuscripts (1844)," p. 352. Emphases original

20. Maurette, *The Forgotten Sense*, p. xiii. Emphasis original.

21. Marx, "Economic and Philosophical Manuscripts (1844)," p. 352. Emphases original.

22. Ibid., p. 348. Emphasis original.

LAY OUT YOUR UNREST

Lightning Source UK Ltd.
Milton Keynes UK
UKHW022137040122
396623UK00005B/52